Prosci Change Management
Certification Program

The ADKAR Model

A pictorial review of Prosci's
3-day certification program

ISBN 978-1-930885-56-1

HD58.8 2008

Prosci
Loveland, CO, USA

© Prosci 2008

Learning Center Publications

D1082567

Hopefully you are now sitting, relaxed, and on your way home. Take a deep breath and feel good that you have successfully completed an intense 3-day experience on managing the people side of change. Many participants leave the certification program feeling like they drank from a fire hose – you may feel the same way!

We would like you to take a minute to come out of the trees and take a look back at the entire forest. The following pages are a pictorial review that is designed as:

- A short read while you are flying back or shortly after returning home.
- A quick reference guide as you get caught up in the busy activities of your daily work.
- A presentation of where to go from here (see pages 48-61).

Day 1

The people side of change

Project teams often ignore the people side of change as they focus on the technical aspects of their solution. They associate technical success with project success. Your mission is to create converging paths that bring together change management and project management to achieve the business objectives of the change.

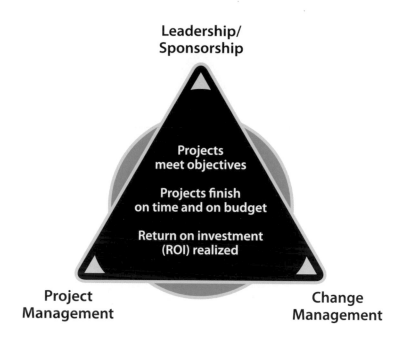

Leadership/
Sponsorship

Projects
meet objectives

Projects finish
on time and on budget

Return on investment
(ROI) realized

Project
Management

Change
Management

Prosci PCT Model

Change initiatives succeed when the foundation elements of leadership, project management, and change management are in place. Prosci's PCT model and PCT Analyzer provide a framework and assessment tool for ensuring that your projects are positioned for success.

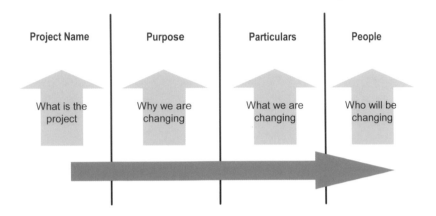

Project Name	Purpose	Particulars	People
What is the project	Why we are changing	What we are changing	Who will be changing

Connecting the people side of change with project success

If the *people* impacted by a project do not support and engage in the change, then the *particulars* of that change, including new processes, systems, or job roles, are not realized. If these *particulars* are not achieved, then we fail to achieve the *purpose* of this project. In short, the business objectives are not met.

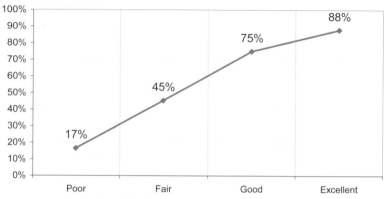

Participants who met or exceeded **OBJECTIVES**

Overall effectiveness of change management program
Data from Prosci's 2007 Best Practices in Change Management benchmarking study
www.change-management.com

Correlation with project objectives

Data from nearly 400 project teams in Prosci's most recent study show that project success (achieving or exceeding objectives) is directly tied to change management effectiveness. This same correlation can be found in Prosci's 2005 study and in research work printed in the McKinsey Quarterly.

LaClair, Jennifer A., and Ravi P. Rao. "Helping Employees Embrace Change." *The McKinsey Quarterly.* 2002 Number 4.

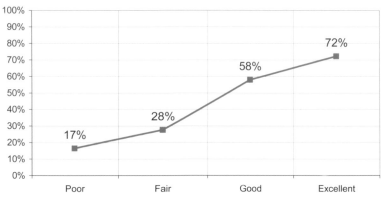

Participants who were on or ahead of *SCHEDULE*

Overall effectiveness of change management program
Data from Prosci's 2007 Best Practices in Change Management benchmarking study
www.change-management.com

Correlation with schedule

Not only do projects meet their objectives with effective change management, they have a greater probability of staying on schedule.

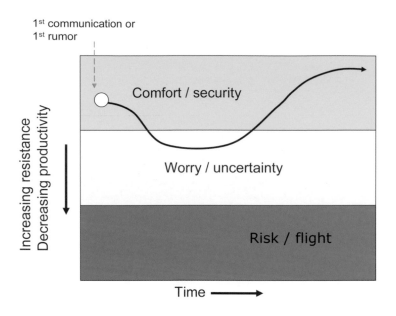

Flight Risk Model

With change, things will likely get worse before they get better. How ***much*** worse, and for ***how long***, depends on how well you manage the people side of the change. Change projects with excellent change management are five times more likely to succeed than projects with poor change management.

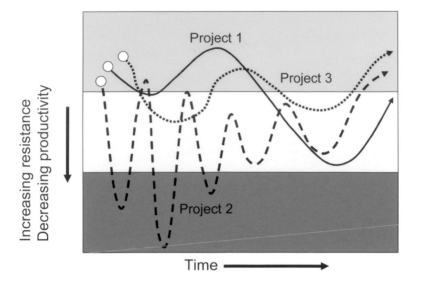

Flight Risk Model

When multiple changes impact your employees, the disruptions in day-to-day operations increase. Poor change management of multiple changes compounds these business risks, which can include a decline in productivity, employee turnover and negative customer impacts.

Implementing an excellent business change without employee engagement is like building a great ship and having no crew. You might stay afloat for a while but you may never leave port.

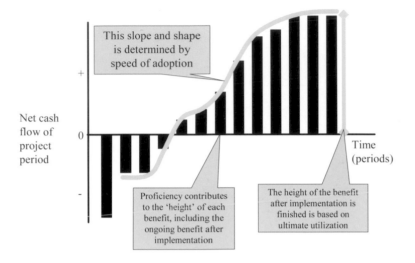

ROI of change management

A common myth is that change management is only about the soft-side of change. In fact, change management is about meeting financial goals that are tied directly to employee speed of adoption, ultimate utilization and proficiency. Next time you are asked by an executive, *"Why change management?,"* you can answer: *"To maximize our overall return on investment and exceed our business objectives for this project."*

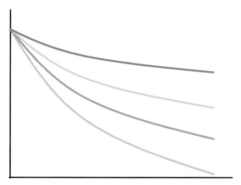

Certainty of
expected ROI
and benefits
from a change

Amount of change to how people do their
jobs – 'people change'

Change management and certainty

The certainty of achieving the expected
benefits from a change is related to the
degree to which the change impacts "how"
people do their jobs. The greater the
impact on people, the greater the
uncertainty that the financial benefits will
be achieved and the greater the need for
change management.

Awareness
Desire
Knowledge
Ability
Reinforcement

The ADKAR Model

Organizations don't change, people change, one person at a time. Understanding how to achieve individual change using ADKAR is critical for achieving organizational change.

The ADKAR® Model

Awareness
Desire
Knowledge
Ability
Reinforcement

Keep these elements in mind when thinking about change:

- *Awareness* of the need for change
- *Desire* to support and participate in the change
- *Knowledge* on how to change
- *Ability* to implement required skills and behaviors
- *Reinforcement* to sustain the change

ADKAR is a registered trademark of Prosci.

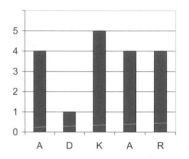 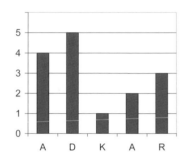

ADKAR profiles

ADKAR profiles can help you understand the change position of both individuals and groups. An individual's barrier point to change is the first ADKAR element that scores a 3 or lower in an ADKAR profile. This knowledge is the missing link between general change management activities and productive management of the people side of change.

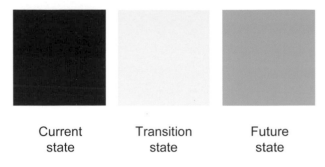

Current state   Transition state   Future state

States of change

Change is represented by three distinct states. The current state has a powerful holding force on employees. The transition state is emotionally charged and chaotic. The future state is often unknown and a source of fear. Project teams and leaders typically operate in a "future state" mindset. Employees live in the current state and will work hard to maintain the status quo. The transition state has the greatest potential for negative impact on an organization.

The concept that "change occurs in three phases" has been well-documented in change management literature for many years including early work by Lewin (Resolving Social Conflicts, 1948), Bridges (Transitions, 1980) and by Beckhard and Harris (Organizational Transitions, 1987).

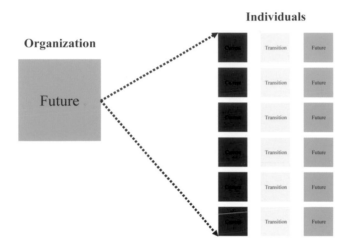

States of change

Although a project team may envision their future state as a singular destination, change is actually realized when each employee moves out of their current state, through a transition state and into his or her unique future state. The collective result of these individual changes produces the organizational change we are striving for with any change project.

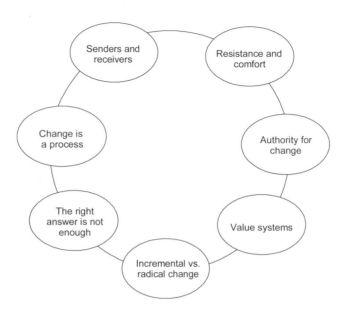

Change concepts

Change theory and conceptual models help us understand the dynamics of change and how we can become better change leaders. Learning about the theory of human and group behavior directly contributes to better change management techniques. As you better understand the "*why*," you will become more effective at the "*how,*" and you will be more skilled when dealing with unique situations.

2007 © Prosci and Bill Cigliano

Senders and receivers

Employees rarely internalize change messages the first time around. They often translate business messages into personal implications and many of the key business messages are lost. Remember to repeat key messages five to seven times.

Resistance and comfort

Don't be surprised by resistance from employees. Resistance is normal. Proactively planning for resistance is a core element of a good change management strategy. Your goal is not to eliminate resistance, but rather to anticipate it and work to mitigate the consequences. With that said, ***persistent*** and ***enduring*** resistance is a threat to the success of a change.

Authority for change

Active and visible sponsorship is the number one success factor for change. Effective sponsorship creates credibility for the project and shows the organization's commitment to the change.

Value systems

Cultural norms, value systems, power distribution and change history are just some of the factors that form the backdrop for change. Some of these factors will work in your favor, whereas others will present obstacles to change. For example, empowered work groups that take ownership for their work – *a quality we desire* – can actually be more resistant to top-down change.

Incremental vs radical change

Change management is not a "one-size fits all" approach. We must customize and scale our change management plans to match the particular change and the attributes of the impacted organization. Good change managers can follow a standard framework for change management while at the same time they scale their activities to match the challenge at hand. Any given change may be incremental to some employees and radical for others.

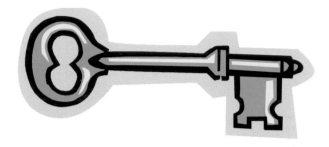

The right answer is not enough

Managers that are convinced they have the right answer can be the worst change leaders – being "right" in no way guarantees employee support and engagement in a change.

2007 Copyright Prosci and Bill Cigliano

Change is a process

Many managers make the mistake that change management is a good meeting or an effective training event. As much as we might like our employees to change instantly, change is a process that occurs over time. In many cases we may need to spend as much time reinforcing change after implementation as we did building awareness of the need for change in the beginning.

Change Management Process

Similar to how ADKAR provides a framework for individual change management, a process is essential for managing change at an organizational level. Prosci's 3-phase process for change management is based on research findings from more than 1000 companies undergoing major change initiatives.

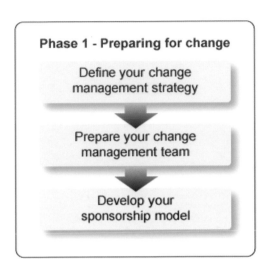

Phase 1 – Preparing for change

Phase 1 of the process requires that you step back and evaluate the change, the organization, your team and the strength of your sponsorship. This work forms the foundation for your change management strategy.

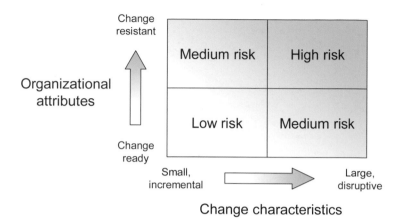

Risk assessment

Each change has unique risks based on the characteristics of the change and the attributes of the impacted organization. Understanding these risks helps us scale our change management plans accordingly.

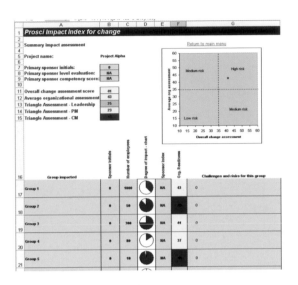

Prosci Impact Index

Assessment tools can help us visualize the strengths and challenges associated with a given change. This data helps us focus on each impacted group and design plans that are specific and relevant for each affected area.

Day 2

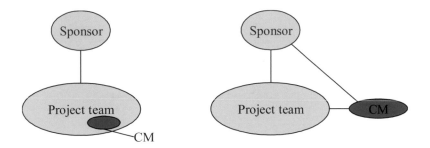

Team structure

By identifying the right team members and the best change management team model, you are beginning the process of integrating change management with project management. You also are ensuring that you will have the right personnel and structure for effectively managing change, both with the project team and with your leadership group.

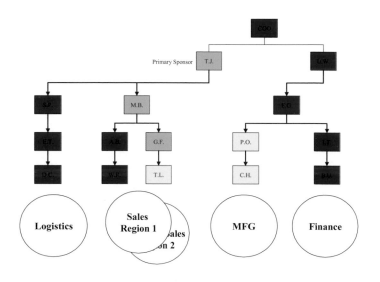

Sponsor assessment diagram

The sponsor assessment diagram is the number one predictor of success for change projects. The colors of this diagram will shift over the life of the project as your primary sponsor and the change management team carefully manage this coalition of leaders.

Phase 2 – Managing change

At some point, analysis and data collection must end and action must begin. The change management plans include:

- *Communications*
- *Sponsorship*
- *Training*
- *Coaching*
- *Resistance management*

At this phase, change management is integrated into the project plan and becomes a formal part of the project.

Communications plan

The best communication plans identify the impacted groups and create key messages appropriate for that group. Good communication plans utilize preferred senders, create two-way communications, and use face-to-face communications whenever possible. Remember to repeat key messages five to seven times.

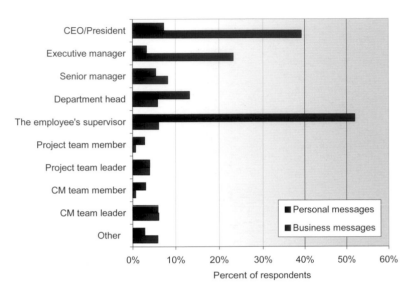

Preferred senders

Research data shows that employees prefer to hear from the *"person in charge"* about why the change is being made and how the change aligns with the vision for the organization. Employees prefer to hear about the personal implications of the change from their direct supervisor. You will be working with each of these groups to enable them to be effective change leaders.

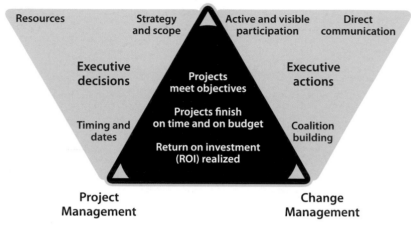

Leadership/
Sponsorship

Resources   Strategy
and scope

Active and visible
participation

Direct
communication

Executive
decisions

Projects
meet objectives

Executive
actions

Timing and
dates

Projects finish
on time and on budget

Coalition
building

Return on investment
(ROI) realized

Project
Management

Change
Management

Sponsor roadmap

Sponsors often associate their role with decision making around strategy, resources and schedule. Great change sponsors also embrace an active and visible role during change. They build coalitions, communicate directly with employees and engage with the project team.

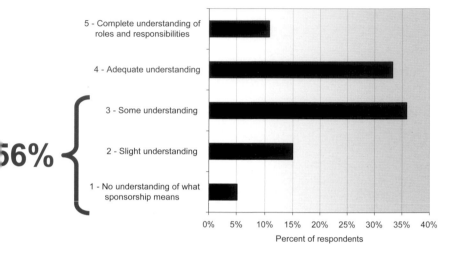

Sponsors and their role

A common reason that business and government leaders do not engage in an active role as change sponsors is that they lack awareness of the need for their participation and they lack an understanding about how to act in the role of a great change sponsor. Remember that you are the sponsor's coach.

Day 3

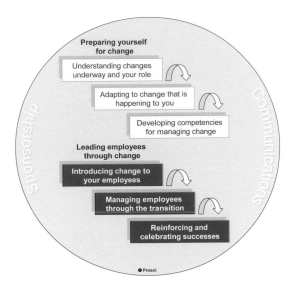

Coaching plan

Managers and supervisors present a unique challenge. While they can be the most resistant group to change, they are recognized in multiple research studies as preferred senders, the best resistance managers, effective communicators and critical liaisons to the project team. In other words, managers and supervisors are the primary gateway for managing change with employees.

Resistance management plan

As much as we may prefer to ignore
resistance to change, planning for
resistance is just as important as planning
for training or communications. We must
know what resistance looks like and how
to equip our managers and supervisors to
manage resistance within their groups.
We need to know when to allow resistance
to "run its course" and when to intervene
in cases of persistent and enduring
resistance.

Training plan

Many aspects of change management are focused on building awareness and desire, but once your employees are on-board and ready to go, they must be equipped with the knowledge and ability to succeed. Training can provide both of these critical elements if it is well-designed and provides employees with opportunities to practice in a safe environment.

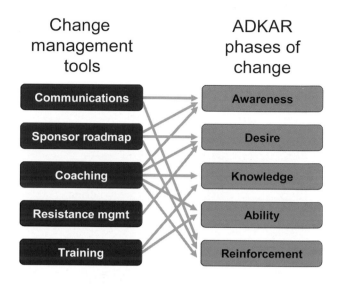

Aligning organizational change management and individual change management

Each change management activity or tool has specific outcomes that can be aligned with the ADKAR model. For example, we communicate to build ***awareness*** of the need for change. We train to develop ***knowledge*** and ***ability***. By aligning activities with desired outcomes, we can both focus and measure our change management work and make adjustments where necessary.

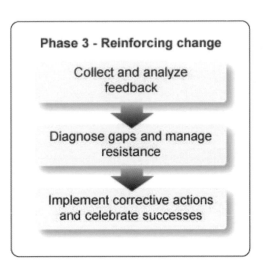

Phase 3

Reinforcing change is not just about making the change stick. It is first making sure that the change is actually taking hold. Compliance audits, performance measurement and resistance management are necessary steps. Once implemented, recognition, rewards and celebrations help sustain the change. Compensation and measurement systems must be aligned with the change.

Change Management Strategy	Change Management Activities	Change Management Outcomes	Business Results
Assess change	Communication	Awareness	On time
Assess org	Sponsorship	Desire	On budget
Assess sponsor model	Training	Knowledge	Achieve business objectives
	Coaching	Ability	
Assess risks and challenges	Resistance management	Reinforcement	- lower costs
Develop special tactics			- increased revenue

The big picture

When you stand back from the entire process, you can see the alignment between your change management strategy work and the ultimate achievement of business results.

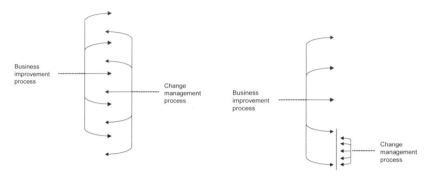

Business improvement process

Change management process

Business improvement process

Change management process

Beginning early

In the unfortunate event that you find yourself applying change management in the middle or end of a project rather than at the beginning, you will be spending a lot of time firefighting and doing damage control. However, even in this situation, the process still works. Take the time to develop your strategy and plans before you are immersed in the immediate problems. It is important that you can stand back and develop a robust assessment and sound approach to the problem.

Prosci Change Management Maturity Model™

Level 5	Organizational Competency	Change management competency is evident in all levels of the organization and is part of the organization's intellectual property and competitive edge	Continuous process improvement in place	Highest profitability and responsiveness
Level 4	Organizational Standards	Organization-wide standards and methods are broadly deployed for managing and leading change	Selection of common approach	↑
Level 3	Multiple Projects	Comprehensive approach for managing change is being applied in multiple projects	Examples of best practices evident	
Level 2	Isolated Projects	Some elements of change management are being applied in isolated projects	Many different tactics used inconsistently	↓
Level 1	Adhoc or Absent	Little or no change management applied	People-dependent without any formal practices or plans	Highest rate of project failure, turnover and productivity loss

Change management maturity model

Prosci's change management maturity model can help you think about your organization's readiness and competency for change. Where is your organization today and what steps would be necessary to build change management competency throughout the organization?

Looking ahead

Next steps

You have successfully finished your certification program. Congratulations and thank you for the energy you applied to this work. Your journey has just begun. The summit lies ahead and you will need to refocus your energies on the challenges before you. Prosci is here to help.

Webinars

Webinars are a free offering provided by Prosci and taught by our Director of Research and Development. These teleconference/web sessions will help you "dig deeper" into change management topics and challenge the way you think about leading change. Invite anyone from your team. Learn more about webinars at:

www.change-management.com/webinars.htm

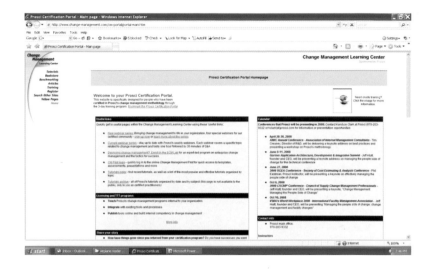

Community building

The certification portal provides you with quick access to webinar logins, tutorials, lessons-learned from other practitioners and direct access to your instructor. This portal is exclusively for you and other Prosci certified practitioners.

Log in at www.change-management.com/cm-portal

Your password is *Prosci*.

Additional products and courses from Prosci

Onsite change management training

Prosci can bring change management training directly to your location.

- **3-day *certification courses*** for your project teams
- ***1-day coaching workshops*** to enable managers to become great change leaders
- ***4-6 hour executive briefings*** that will help you build great sponsorship

Call us to schedule onsite courses and to learn about our train-the-trainer program.

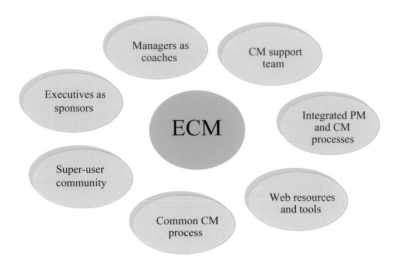

Enterprise change management (ECM)

When you are ready to deploy change management across your organization, Prosci offers three programs:

- ECM Vision program
- ECM Lab workshop
- ECM Deployment program

The ECM Vision program is conducted via teleconference and is offered free for your organization to help get the process started.

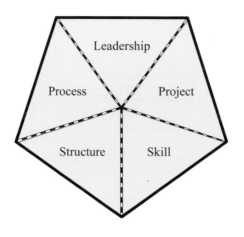

Prosci's ECM strategy map

Prosci's unique approach to enterprise change management enables you to create a comprehensive deployment map that addresses:

- leadership development
- project management
- skill building and competency development
- change management structure
- process standardization

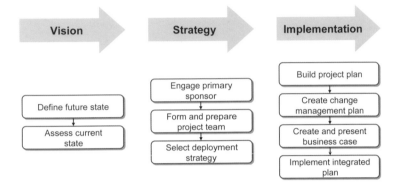

Prosci's ECM Deployment process

When you are ready for implementation, we can help you refine your strategy and develop concrete deployment plans for ECM. The ECM deployment process is based on research and experience with clients and provides structure to the project you are taking on – that of building your change management competency at all levels in the organization.

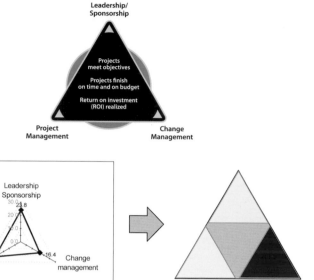

Prosci's PCT Analyzer

Prosci's latest online application, the PCT Analyzer, allows you to assess the health of multiple projects using the PCT model. With this web-based tool you can identify strengths and gaps across your organization. This powerful tool also provides insight as to the biggest problem areas within each project and how you can remedy those issues. See: www.change-management.com/pct-analyzer.htm for more information.

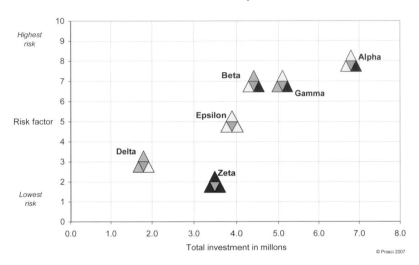

Investment vs risk analysis

Prosci's Change Portfolio Management

Once you have mastered the PCT Model you are ready to take the next step toward *Change Portfolio Management.* Imagine the reaction of your executive team when they see the risk vs. investment graph of their most critical strategic initiatives. Bringing this level of insight to your leadership team will help them identify gaps and resolve barriers to project success.

Books and research reports

Prosci offers many support resources including books, reports and assessment tools. These are available as single products or through volume discounts. You can also secure a site license that includes these products. See www.change-management.com.bookstore.htm for more information.

Toolkits, online applications and site licenses

Prosci provides the most comprehensive set of toolkits and online applications for change management. These can be purchased in a single-user license format or with a company-wide site license.

Thank you for your commitment and time this week. We look forward to hearing from you.

Sincerely,

The Prosci Team
Your place to go for change management.

Prosci
www.change-management.com
970-203-9332

Topic reference